ANIMALS AT RISK

Sea Otters In Danger

BY ELLA MINEO

Gareth Stevens
Publishing

Please visit our website, www.garethstevens.com. For a free color catalog of all our high-quality books, call toll free 1-800-542-2595 or fax 1-877-542-2596.

Library of Congress Cataloging-in-Publication Data

Mineo, Ella.
Sea otters in danger / by Ella Mineo.
  p. cm. — (Animals at risk)
Includes index.
ISBN 978-1-4339-9170-7 (pbk.)
ISBN 978-1-4339-9171-4 (6-Pack)
ISBN 978-1-4339-9169-1 (library binding)
1. Sea otter — Juvenile literature. 2. Endangered species — Juvenile literature. I. Title.
QL737.C25 M56 2014
599.7695—dc23

First Edition

Published in 2014 by
Gareth Stevens Publishing
111 East 14th Street, Suite 349
New York, NY 10003

Copyright © 2014 Gareth Stevens Publishing

Designer: Andrea Davison-Bartolotta
Editor: Therese M. Shea

Photo credits: Cover, p. 1 Danita Delimont/Gallo Images/Getty Images; pp. 4, 6, 7, 8, 10, 13, 20 iStockphoto/Thinkstock; p. 5 Katherine Welles/Shutterstock.com; p. 9 Jean-Edouard Rozey/Shutterstock.com; p. 11 Tom & Pat Leeson/Photo Researchers/Getty Images; p. 12 Doug Steakley/Lonely Planet Images/Getty Images; p. 15 Heather Dillon/Shutterstock.com; p. 17 Stan Wayman/Time Life Pictures/Getty Images; p. 18 Oli Scarff/Getty Images; p. 19 Elliotte Rusty Harold/Shutterstock.com; p. 21 (sea otter) bierchen/Shutterstock.com, (seaweed) worldswildlifewonders/Shutterstock.com, (sea urchin) arguta/Shutterstock.com, (elepant seal) creativex/Shutterstock.com, (horn shark) Mark Conlin/Oxford Scientific/Getty Images, (kelp crab) Daniel Gotshall/Visuals Unlimited/Getty Images.

Printed in the United States of America

CPSIA compliance information: Batch #CS13GS: For further information contact Gareth Stevens, New York, New York at 1-800-542-2595.

CONTENTS

Cute, Furry, and in Danger..4

Floating Through Life...6

Seafood, Please!...8

Clever Creatures 10

Pups!... 12

Fur Treaty... 14

A Terrible Accident 16

Other Otters... 18

Keystone Species... 20

Glossary... 22

For More Information... 23

Index... 24

Words in the glossary appear in **bold** type the first time they are used in the text.

CUTE, FURRY, AND IN DANGER

Sea otters live in the freezing waters of the North Pacific Ocean near the coasts of western North America and eastern Russia. Unlike most sea **mammals**, otters don't have a layer of fat to keep them warm. Instead, they have very thick fur.

At one time, there may have been more than 300,000 sea otters. However, people hunted sea otters for their fur for many years. By the early 1900s, there were fewer than 2,000 sea otters left!

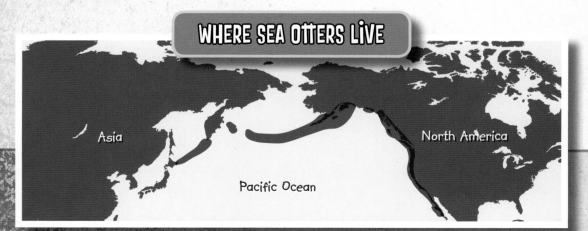

WHERE SEA OTTERS LIVE

Asia

North America

Pacific Ocean

 Few animals in the ocean—or on Earth—are as cute as sea otters!

WILD FACTS

Sea otters belong to the weasel family.

FLOATING THROUGH LIFE

Sea otters' **dense** fur allows them to spend most of their lives in water. They eat and sleep floating on their back. Sometimes they float in groups. They may use seaweed as a kind of bed!

A sea otter uses its webbed back feet like paddles to get around. It uses its tail to turn. Sea otters are excellent divers, too. They can dive 200 feet (61 m) looking for food. And they're always looking for food!

WILD FACTS
Sea otter fur is the densest fur of any animal on Earth!

A sea otter's nose and ears close when it dives underwater.

SEAFOOD, PLEASE!

Sea otters eat a lot. A sea otter weighing about 60 pounds (27 kg) may eat 12 pounds (5 kg) of food every day! They like to eat many kinds of sea creatures, including mussels, crabs, fish, snails, **sea urchins**, octopuses, clams, and **abalones**.

Otters can hold their breath up to 4 minutes while diving for food. They may use their **whiskers** to find food in dark, deep waters. These long hairs are **sensitive** like those of a cat.

WILD FACTS
Most sea otters are about 4 feet (1.2 m) long.

When a sea otter finds a tasty treat, it enjoys it while lying on its back.

Some of otters' favorite meals are crustaceans (kruhs-TAY-shunz), which are sea animals with shells. Sea otters do something when they eat that's rarely seen in other animals. You might see a sea otter with a crustacean in one hand and a rock in the other. It lays the rock on its stomach and pounds the shell against the rock, breaking it open.

Only a few other animals use tools when they eat—some birds and **primates**, including people! After eating, sea otters carefully clean themselves.

This hungry sea otter tries to open a clam.

PUPS!

Mother sea otters have one baby, or pup, at a time. They give birth in the water. Sea otter pups have some hair and can float, but they can't swim. A pup stays on its mother's stomach while she paddles around on her back. It begins to swim on its own when it's about 2 months old.

Sea otters don't make many sounds, but mothers and pups may call to each other. Pups make a squealing noise when they're separated from their mother.

▼ A mother sea otter and her baby swim in waters near Alaska.

WILD FACTS

A mother sea otter tried to climb into a boat to rescue her pup when scientists took it from the water for a time.

A person may have fewer than 200,000 hairs on their whole head. Sea otter fur has as many as 1 million hairs per square inch (6.5 sq cm)! Long ago, people used otter fur for clothing, such as gloves and coats. By the early 1900s, some people realized sea otters would soon be **extinct**.

In 1911, Canada, Japan, Russia, and the United States agreed to the International Fur Seal **Treaty**, stopping most sea otter hunting. This helped the population increase to perhaps as many as 150,000 today.

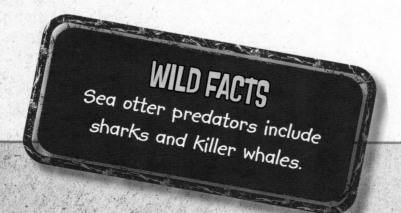

WILD FACTS
Sea otter predators include sharks and killer whales.

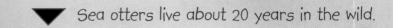
Sea otters live about 20 years in the wild.

A Terrible Accident

Sea otter numbers are still much lower than they once were. Otters are sometimes caught in nets meant for fish and other sea creatures. They drown if they can't come up for air.

Sea otters face other dangers, too. For example, a ship spilled millions of gallons of oil near Alaska in 1989. Oil has a bad effect on sea otter fur. Oil makes the fur clump and lose its waterproof features. About 2,800 sea otters froze to death because of the oil spill.

WILD FACTS
A group of resting sea otters is called a raft. A raft may have more than 100 otters.

Polluted shores also have bad effects on sea otters and other sea creatures. Pollution can get into the water through rain and wind.

Other Otters

There are 13 **species** of otters. All have long, thin bodies and are excellent swimmers. The smallest otter is the Asian small-clawed otter. The sea otter is the largest. These two are also the only species that catch food with their hands instead of their mouths.

Besides sea otters, other species are in trouble. The giant otter, marine otter, hairy-nosed otter, and southern river otter are in danger of extinction. Sadly, otters' friendliness can make them easy to hunt.

ASIAN SMALL-CLAWED OTTER

These river otters look different from their Asian small-clawed cousins on the opposite page.

KEYSTONE SPECIES

Some otters have been raised in zoos and **released** back into the wild to help their numbers increase. However, this doesn't answer many problems. Otters' natural **habitats** need to be pollution-free, and illegal hunting must be stopped.

A keystone species is one on which many animals rely. Sea otters are a keystone species. They eat sea urchins that eat seaweed. Without otters, there might be too many urchins and too little seaweed. An unhealthy ocean would have a terrible effect on people, too.

An Ocean Food Web

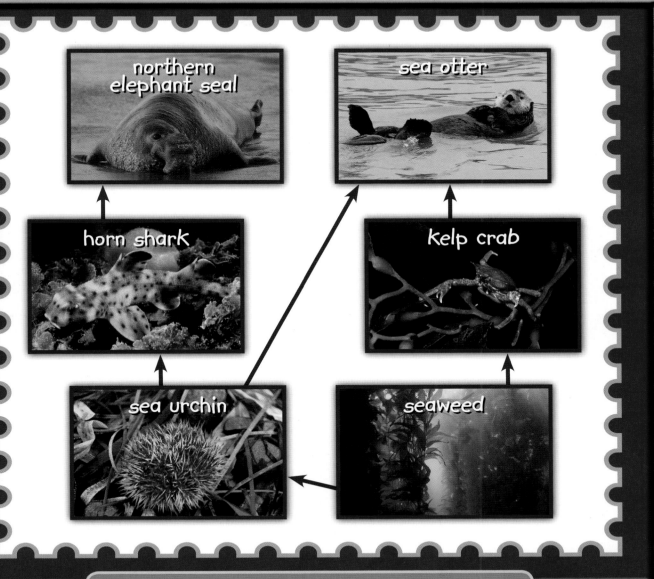

Follow the arrows to see how some ocean animals depend on each other for food.

GLOSSARY

abalone: a shellfish with an ear-shaped shell

dense: packed very closely together

extinct: no longer living

habitat: the natural place where an animal or plant lives

mammal: a warm-blooded animal that has a backbone and hair, breathes air, and feeds milk to its young

primate: any animal from the group that includes humans, apes, and monkeys

release: to set free

sea urchin: a small sea animal with a soft body in a spiny shell

sensitive: able to sense or feel changes in surroundings

species: a group of plants or animals that are all of the same kind

treaty: an agreement between countries

whisker: a long hair growing near the mouth of some mammals, such as cats and otters

For More Information

Books

King, Zelda. *Sea Otters*. New York, NY: PowerKids Press, 2012.

Leardi, Jeanette. *Southern Sea Otters: Fur-tastrophe Avoided*. New York, NY: Bearport Publishing, 2008.

Lockwood, Sophie. *Sea Otters*. Chanhassen, MN: Child's World, 2006.

Websites

Fact Sheet: Sea Otter
www.defenders.org/sea-otter/basic-facts
Read facts about sea otters and learn what you can do to help them.

Sea Otter
animals.nationalgeographic.com/animals/mammals/sea-otter/
Hear what sea otters sound like on this National Geographic website.

Publisher's note to educators and parents: Our editors have carefully reviewed these websites to ensure that they are suitable for students. Many websites change frequently, however, and we cannot guarantee that a site's future contents will continue to meet our high standards of quality and educational value. Be advised that students should be closely supervised whenever they access the Internet.

INDEX

Asian small-clawed otter 18, 19

baby 12, 13

back 6, 9, 12

clothing 14

crustaceans 10

dangers 16, 18

divers 6, 7, 8

food 6, 8, 18, 21

food web 21

fur 4, 6, 14, 16

giant otter 18

habitats 20

hairy-nosed otter 18

hunting 4, 14, 18, 20

International Fur Seal Treaty 14

keystone species 20

marine otter 18

mothers 12, 13

North America 4

North Pacific Ocean 4

oil spill 16

pollution 17, 20

predators 14

pups 12, 13

raft 16

river otter 18, 19

Russia 4, 14

seaweed 6, 20, 21

species 18, 20

tail 6

tools 10

weasel family 5

webbed back feet 6

whiskers 8